RHYME &
REASON

Written by Sylvia Turner
Illustrated by Lisa Smith

Collins Educational
An imprint of HarperCollins*Publishers*

Contents

INTRODUCTION

When you read poetry, do you notice that some poems rhyme, while others have no rhymes at all? Do you sense the rhythm in a poem? One might have a regular beat, almost like a song. Another seems to stay closer to the rhythms of natural speech. Can you spot words that have been picked for sound as well as for meaning?

The poems in this book show you some of the traditional forms of poetry and each form is explained. Some came to Britain from other parts of the world, which is why they have Italian, French, Spanish or Japanese names.

There is also a section of commonly used terms to help you understand more about what makes poetry work. Writing poetry yourself is the best way of understanding it, though, and it is hoped that enjoying this book will make you want to try your hand.

SHAPED VERSE OR CONCRETE POETRY

A complete poem whose shape represents the subject of the poem: a house poem shaped like a house, or a cat poem shaped like a cat. The line lengths are chosen for no other reason than to suit the shape. *Family Tree* and *Paper Boats* are examples of shaping a poem.

In most traditional forms of poetry, the number of syllables in a line sets its length. So, long lines have more syllables and words than short lines, and look longer. Even lines have the same number of syllables.

Family Tree

Two Uncles
three Aunts,
two Margarets, a Mary,
(one with a chin that's decidedly hairy).
Two Grandads, one Grandma, and Step-Grandpa Joe
(who wears a wig if you want to know).
Great Uncles and Aunts, a Father, a Mother.
Eight cousins, one In-law,
two Sisters, a Brother. Don't ask me who else…
Count them?
I'm
sunk!
But
it's
my
family
tree
and
that
makes
me the trunk!

Paper Boats

I
made
myself a paper
boat and launched it in
a sheltered moat, shallow and calm
to left and right, no puff of wind: my boat sat tight, refused to sail
or even twirl. I saw an edge begin to curl, slowly and unfolding,
opening out, for the fish to read the news, no doubt. It
honoured me, stuck on this bank, with a wet
bob-curtsey, then it sank.

I
built
myself a sturdier
craft, waterproof joints
both fore and aft. I straightened
the sail then checked each fold, waiting until
the wind took hold. I watched it spin, then dip and lift, its mast still
proud - could that boat shift! Like the winner in a yachting
race it cut through the waves while I gave chase
along the towpath, unsurprised to find my
show-off had capsized.

I
shaped
a ship of
words alone –
folded dreams, anchored
to stone. I sent my ship twice round the moon
while water lapped a distant tune. With
magic joints no axe can sever,
a boat like mine should
float for ever!

COUPLET

Two lines of verse which often rhyme and sometimes have a regular rhythm.

On the Beach is made up of three rhymed couplets, with a break between each. The lines are even in length and quite short. Each has a count of eight syllables.

Quick March is different. The couplets rhyme, but the lines are uneven: some long, some short. There are no breaks.

Baby Mallard is also made up of rhymed couplets. The lines are longer, but still even.

On the Beach

Together, hand in hand,
we hop across damp sand

so people way behind
will be puzzled to find

in the glimmering heat
the prints of two left feet.

9

Quick March

We like our lollipop lady,
Mrs Cady,
who once served in the police force.
She stands square as a horse
to stop any truck, no matter how big the load,
just to see us across the road.
If a car dares to toot a horn, she'll pause,
stride across and stun the driver with some clause
learnt by heart from the Traffic Act.
It's a fact!
Even if a posh chauffeur blared and made a fuss
Mrs Cady would still favour us.

Baby Mallard

A pipsqueak harlequin, lollipop-neat,
pads after Amy on paper-thin feet;

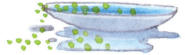

dabbles for duckweed, a saucer its pond,
scrabbles up Amy's sleeve, trick vagabond.

Now weary, this fluffball with flip-flop tread
sees Amy's slipper, scuffles into bed.

TRIPLET AND TERCET

A triplet is a stanza of three lines, and a tercet is a complete poem of three lines. Both can be rhymed or unrhymed.

Heatwave is a <u>haiku</u>, a complete poem in three lines that creates a clear picture in very few words. The lines do not rhyme, and each one has an exact number of syllables: 5 in the first line, 7 in the second and 5 in the third. The haiku is a Japanese form, and well suited to the Japanese language which is unstressed.

Insect on a Train is made up of two <u>envelope triplets</u>. Each stanza has three lines, with lines 1 and 3 rhyming. This makes an envelope, or an enclosure, round the second line.

Katy Skipping is made up of <u>rhymed triplets</u>. In each stanza, all three lines rhyme. The rhyme changes from stanza to stanza.

Aquarium is a <u>terza rima</u>, an Italian form made up of envelope triplets with even lines. The middle line of the first stanza rhymes with lines 1 and 3 of the next, and so on throughout the poem. The poem ends with a rhymed couplet.

Heatwave

My shadow's grounded
on hot tarmac, arms flapping
to keep itself cool.

Insect on a Train

Inside our speeding train
an idle gnat flitters
down aisles and back again.

Small as a grain of salt,
will it know to change gear
when we pull to a halt?

Katy Skipping

Tip-tap-toe on the tarmac track,
Katy's shoes flash snappy and black
click-clacking like a jumping jack.

Down swings the rope, swish on the ground,
swoops overhead without a sound,
a mill-wheel lashing round and round.

Katy, still jumping, makes no slips,
keeping count through whispering lips;
one, two, three, her skipping rope flips;

leaping over a mountain stream,
tip-tap-toe where the North star's beam
lends magic to her skipping-dream.

Aquarium

When Dad needed to clean the slimy tank,
I took my goldfish to the pond and thought
as I watched them slip away from the bank

how pleased they'd be tomorrow when I brought
them home to clear glass and fresh waterweed…
But next afternoon, could those fish be caught?

I trawled cunning nets, tempted them to feed.
Then one warm day I saw a heron stroll
in and stand there, its leg a single reed,

its sharp beak set to gulp my poor fish whole!
Next spring, though, I saw four golden shapes loom
in the pond, unharmed – too big for any bowl.

My fish had swelled, glad of the extra room,
scales beaming tangerine through dusky gloom.

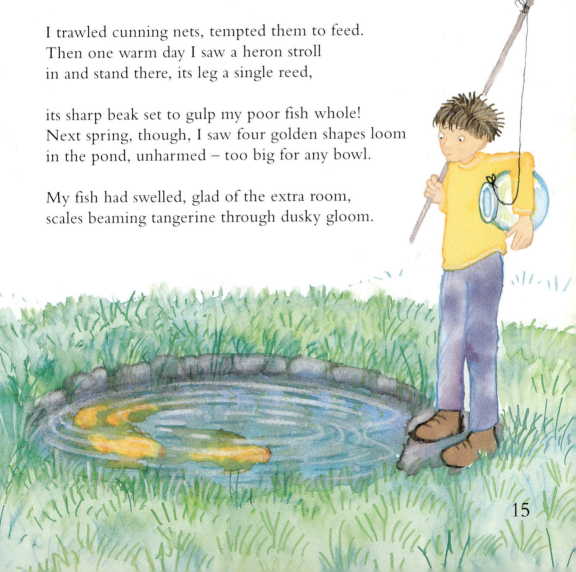

QUATRAIN

A stanza or a complete poem of four lines, which may rhyme or not.

Science is a complete four-lined poem with lines 2 and 4 rhyming.

Miss Willoughby has a strong rhythm drumming throughout the poem: **dum**-di-di, **dum**-di-di. This is the same rhythm as *Hickory Dickory*. When a line follows this pattern, it is known as a <u>double dactyl</u>. Lines 4 and 8 stop short in this sort of poem.

Swing Bridge has very short lines of only four syllables in each.

Party Piece is a <u>Clerihew</u>, a fun poem of four lines made up of two couplets. The first line should end with the name of a famous person, though the example does not. The form was invented by Edmund Clerihew Bentley and named after him.

April Weather has four lines that rhyme alternately. This is the most common form of all poetry. Such quatrains are much favoured by writers of hymns and carols.

Science

If the world really spins
as it hurtles through space,
how come, when I jump up,
I land in the same place?

Miss Willoughby

Jiggery Pokery
silly Miss Willoughby
loses her glasses so
can't see a speck.

Rings the police station
unnecessarily.
Where are her spectacles?
Strung round her neck!

Swing Bridge

The river's wide
with rocky banks.
The bridge is long
and made of planks;

just wide enough
for me to stride,
gripping the wire
on either side.

A floor of slats
with oblong holes,
legs as long as
telegraph poles.

The oddest bridge
I've ever seen,
springier than
a trampoline.

Party Piece

Andy Meers,
claims he has double-jointed ears.
He gathers an audience to watch the display.
Do his ears waggle? No way.

April Weather

The day my grandad's hat flew free
and ma's umbrella whipped inside out,
gales blew so wild that every tree
shook giant fists and flew about.

But by the time I found my kite
and fixed its tail and wound new string
the wind had dropped, the sun shone bright
and white clouds puffed; I heard birds sing.

With swimming things stuffed in my pack
I set out for the pool, but then
the sun went in, the wind blew back
to shake and crack the trees again.

Thinking of kites I ran home quick
until I realised calm and cool,
that this was just another trick –
the weather playing April Fool.

QUINTET

A stanza or poem of five lines.

Market Gardener is made up of two cinquains. A cinquain, which can also be a complete poem, has five lines, each with an exact syllable count: 2 in the first line, 4 in the second, 6 in the third, 8 in the fourth, and back to 2 in the fifth. Invented by an American, Adelaide Crapsey, it could be called the English language version of a Japanese tanka.

Backyard is a tanka, which is simply a haiku with an unrhymed couplet tagged on to the end. Each of the final lines have seven syllables which gives the whole poem a total of 31 syllables.

Trust is a Sicilian quintet, a five-lined poem, with lines rhymed alternately.

Candyfloss is a quintilla, a complete poem that uses two rhymes only and never ends in a couplet. A quintilla can also be a stanza. It is a Spanish form from the sixteenth century.

Couch Potato is a limerick, a humorous poem that pokes fun at people and things. Most people are familiar with limericks. Lines 1, 2 and 5 rhyme with each other; lines 3 and 4 rhyme with each other.

Market Gardener

He stacks
his bike high, crates
jam-packed on handlebars,
sacked potatoes, boxed carrots, beans,
shallots…

Don't breathe
when he glides past,
rickety pile jumping
on the cobbles. One puff and he'll
capsize.

21

Backyard

A hundred raindrops
hang still on the washing line.
Down comes a bluetit
and zip! Pearls scatter across
the yard. A broken necklace.

Trust

In our garden pond, three glossy perch lie
low. I'd show you, but they only come out
of hiding for my brother. You know why?
He found them gasping during last year's drought
and saved them, before the canal ran dry.

22

Candyfloss

Glossy, and light as a balloon,
my gift for mum smelt sweetly pink.
On the coach home, watching it shrink,
I felt as though I'd lost the moon.
A molten lump – so very soon?

Couch Potato

In the next house but one lives Old Nellie
who squanders her life watching telly.
Since she never goes out
but just lazes about
all her muscles have turned soft as jelly.

23

FREE VERSE

This form of poetry has no strict rules about
rhyming, the length of lines, or how stanzas should
be arranged. Because of this, people often think it
is easier to write free verse, but many find it much
harder. The poet has important choices to make:
where to end each line, how to arrange the stanzas.
The inner ear must be trusted, for this kind of
poem has the gentle rhythm of speech, never a
noticeable beat. Yet it does not sound like speech,
nor does it read like a story. Even though the lines
do not rhyme, each word is picked with care,
especially at the end of a line.

No-one is certain who first started to write free
verse, but poets who choose this form want to be
free of restrictions set by tradition, including
subject matter.

Touch

Baby hands are tiny,
pouched silky skin,
creased where
fingers bend;
pearly nails clear
as sweet wrappers.

Thread a finger
into the fist;
the fierce grip
will surprise you.

Old people's hands
are delicately blotched,
as if pressed flowers
had been placed between
the leaves of skin,
layered there
centuries back
for safekeeping.

To hold an old hand
is like grasping
crumpled-up paper.

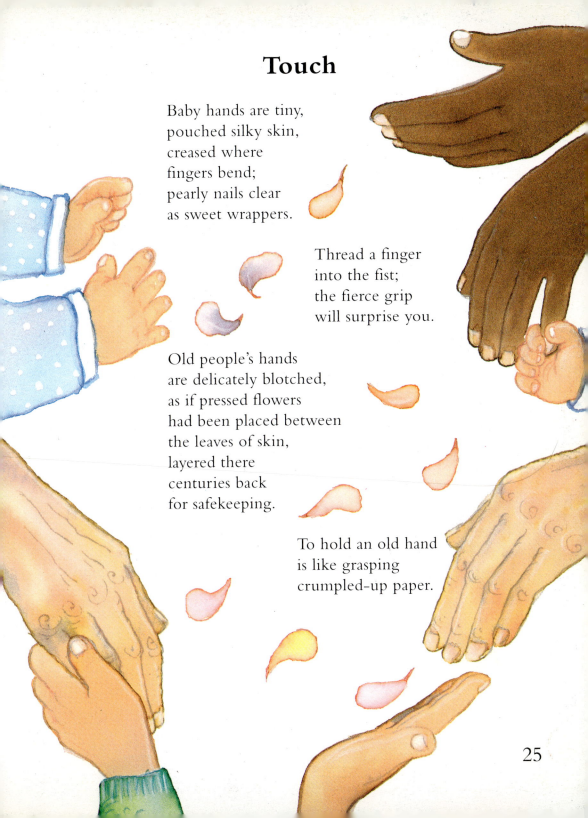

Guessing Game

You can roll it into a telescope,
    cut it into squares, tear it,
      make a Möbius strip if you know how.

You can fold it into flower shapes,
    or triangular-limbed frogs,
      birds with wings to flap.

You can rule lines on it,
    write a poem,
      paint pictures.

But you'd find it hard
    building your own home with it,
      walls fragile as dried leaves,

first grinding wood in your own jaws
    until pulped delicate as tissue,
      shaping it into rooms for your family.

Such a home hangs from my woodshed ceiling,
    like a misplaced fir cone –
      but for the dwellers zooming about
      in their striped suits.

Architect in the Park

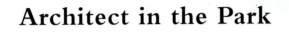

The play area is parched.
A bottle-throw from the ruin,
a small silk-clad Hindu girl
is quietly building a castle.
Scooping dust from arid ground,
she sculpts a dome
flawless as a lotus bell.

She finds burnt-out matchsticks,
pebbles, bottle tops;
to her, agates, bloodstones,
ebony, marble, gold.
Soon, amber chimneys
stud the curved roof.
Four slender minarets stand guard,
dwarfing withered trees.
This summer, drought
turns logs to tinder;
fire makes charcoal skeletons
of timber climbing-frames.

The play area is parched, unmajestic.
Yet, with the composure of an empress,
this small silk-clad Hindu girl
rises to her feet, serenely surveying
her miniature Taj Mahal.

27

SESTET

A stanza of six lines, often the second part of a sonnet.

John Appleby and *Juggler* use <u>rime couée</u>, a stanza with two long lines and one short line, repeated. The long lines are rhymed couplets, the short lines rhyme with each other.

Curling is a <u>Burns stanza</u>. The longer lines, 1, 2, 3 and 5, rhyme with each other and the shorter lines, 4 and 6, rhyme with each other. This form is difficult to write, but Robert Burns, for whom it is named, was skilled at it.

Juggler

"People with sense would skedaddle,"
he yells from his lofty saddle,
    setting three clubs ablaze
to whirl overhead. But we like
the wobble of his one-wheeled bike,
    his daft slap-happy ways.

Eyes in a spin, seeing double,
he's kidding us he's in trouble.
    Up shoots an apple: weird,
how he pedals round underneath,
dinner-fork sprouting from his teeth…
    Chock! One green apple, speared.

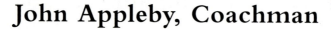

John Appleby, Coachman

(the first man ever to fly, 1853)

Sir George's plane had one wing and a tail.
He prepared to launch it across the dale;
        a stringless kite.
Too weighty himself to fly the machine
George summoned his coachman, thin as a bean,
        to test its flight.

John disliked being a human spider
without a lifeline in that frail glider
        crossing the sky.
When the kite at last landed, out he crawled;
"I was hired to drive," he angrily bawled,
        "and not to fly!"

Never guessing that his own humble name,
John Appleby, would achieve lasting fame
        in history,
he gave in his notice, quit his station
and stormed off on foot, his destination
        sheer mystery.

Curling

At the lake's edge my friend yells "GO!"
Our ice-blocks hurled, we stand tiptoe
to watch our missiles graze thin snow
                    across the rink.
Beyond bare trees the sun dips low;
                    the lake gleams pink.

Both ice-chunks spin and gently slide
across the lake but soon collide,
veer apart to pick up a glide
                    that seems pre-planned,
like spaceships from the moon's dark side
                    come in to land.

Well-wrapped against the biting chill
with frosted breath we hold quite still,
sensing with a shimmering thrill
                    the owl-like hoot
as ice skims ice, an eerie trill,
                    clear as a flute.

OCTAVE

A stanza or poem of eight lines; also the first part of a sonnet.

Borrowed Hat and *Stiltwalker* are made up of two quatrains which rhyme, though the rhymed lines do not always come in a regular order. This form is known as <u>rispetto</u>.

Eclipse is an <u>ottava rima</u>, an Italian form which can be a stanza or a complete poem. Lines 1, 3 and 5 rhyme; lines 2, 4 and 6 rhyme; lines 7 and 8 are a couplet.

Borrowed Hat

I loved Aunt Amy's wedding hat
with flower patterns stitched in gold,
its velvet smooth as any cat –
so beautiful to stroke and hold.

Aunt Amy took it off her head.
"Here – you can have it," Amy said.
"Oh, no," I told her. "That's not fair."
"Well, then – let's say it's ours to share."

Eclipse

We're in the window outstaring the moon,

round as a melon, rind no longer trim

but caving in like a perished balloon.

The smoky smudge now softening the rim

spreads, leaving a blazing banana, soon

to vanish. A gold haze, then all is dim;

the moon's in shadow – but what a disguise!

An earthy potato with crater eyes.

Stiltwalker

See him perched on that pillar box,
long trousers gathered to his thighs.
Straps all unbuckled, he unlocks
his goalpost legs and down he flies.

Even now our walking steeple
can't quite merge with humdrum people;
like my dad, perhaps, but older,
giant chopsticks on one shoulder.

ACROSTIC

Grandfather Clock is an acrostic. The first letter of each line of this kind of poem spells a word when read downwards. The word is often the title.

Usually an acrostic has no rhyme. It will be as long as the word or words used, and it will be broken into the same number of stanzas as the number of words.

Grandfather Clock

Grey-faced, I stare along the hallway,
Rigid, with a narrow door to my innards.
A wobbly brass catch opens me up.
Not many know how to turn it. Inside my
Darkness hangs a metal pendulum,
Forever swinging from side to side.
A weighted chain, looped round cogs, makes me
Tick, notch after notch. Someone must
Heave the chain to raise that weight
Every twenty-four hours, without fail.
Remember to wind me, before time runs out.

Crafted two hundred years ago yet
Look how sturdily I stand,
Older than any living person.
Crotchety, but as accurate as the sun.
Know this: I am the heartbeat of the house.

BLANK VERSE

This is a flexible form of poetry that is particularly suited to English speech patterns. Although it does not sound exactly like spoken English, it works well as dialogue and Shakespeare used it to great effect in his dramas.

Blank verse is also particularly suitable for long narrative poems. Some famous long blank verse poems are Milton's *Paradise Lost*, Wordsworth's *The Prelude* and Tennyson's *Idylls of the King*.

The lines in blank verse are arranged evenly, usually ten syllables to a line, with a regular pulse throughout.

Stranded Spider

It's time they designed a new type of bath

  with built-in ladders for spiders to climb,

    and arrows that say: Turn left at the plug.

So, faced with white cliffs on every side

    that hairy spider now skidding about

could skedaddle back to its hidey-hole.

        Then I'd turn on the taps and have my bath

    instead of loitering, playing for time.

REFRAIN

An entire line repeated elsewhere in a poem.

Edge of the Ocean is a <u>pantoum</u>. This form of complete poem comes from Malaya. A pantoum is often entertaining and light. At first glance, it looks like a series of simple four-lined stanzas. But the refrains are arranged unlike any other poetry, and they obey a strict pattern. Working it out is like doing a puzzle.

Two Great-Great-Uncles on the Merry-go-Round is a <u>villanelle</u>. This is a poem of six stanzas, five of them tercets and one a quatrain ending in a rhyming couplet. The lines add up to 19, but many are the same, and obey a certain pattern. This is another puzzle to work out.

Downhill Roller Skaters is a <u>kyrielle</u>, a French form of complete poem from the Middle Ages. The last line of the first stanza reappears as the last line of every stanza.

Water Recycler is a <u>triolet</u>, which is an eight-lined poem with several repeated lines. Lines 1, 4 and 7 are the same; lines 1 and 2 are repeated as lines 7 and 8.

Edge of the Ocean

The shambling sea
juggles with bones
slops on the quay,
slips over stones.

Juggles with bones
slaps against rocks,
slips over stones,
soaks my new socks.

Slaps against rocks,
licks ticklish toes,
soaks my new socks
splashes my nose.

Licks ticklish toes;
salt-stinging spray
splashes my nose
then sneaks away.

Salt-stinging spray
wets half the beach
then sneaks away,
shrinks out of reach.

Wets half the beach,
slops on the quay,
shrinks out of reach –
the shambling sea.

41

Two Great-Great-Uncles on the Merry-go-Round

Long before roller coasters hit the fair,
when kids had to pedal to make rides spin,
a rickety racket pummelled the air.

There were tigers to mount, a sedan chair,
wooden hyenas with seats made of tin,
long before rollercoasters hit the fair.

Ned sat on a tiger with cardboard hair;
Tom, a lion with a lop-sided grin.
A rickety racket pummelled the air.

They pedalled and pedalled without a care.
The roundabout whirled. Thrill tingled the skin,
long before roller coasters hit the fair.

The bell! On they pedalled, fast as they dare.
"STOP!" called the boss bawling over the din.
A rickety racket pummelled the air.

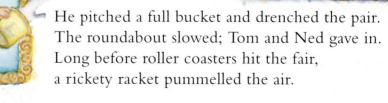

He pitched a full bucket and drenched the pair.
The roundabout slowed; Tom and Ned gave in.
Long before roller coasters hit the fair,
a rickety racket pummelled the air.

Downhill Roller-Skaters

Skates angled wide, they clonk uphill
then about-turn, once at the top,
letting the wheels roll as they will,
ready to grab the rail to stop.

Halfway down and hot from the climb
one says, "Let's buy a lollipop!"
They roll on down in record time,
ready to grab at the rail to stop.

The hill steepens, they pick up speed,
helter-skelter towards the shop,
the girl in red taking the lead,
ready to grab the rail to stop.

Water Recycler

He tips out last night's bottle, hating waste,
into his saucepan to boil today's eggs.
He tips out last night's bottle, hating waste,
swears it makes no difference to the taste.
Now he lowers a teabag, neatly placed,
to make himself a drink from the dregs.
He empties last night's bottle, hating waste,
into his saucepan to boil today's eggs.

43

SONNET

A 14-lined poem with several traditional patterns of rhyming. It is usually in two parts, an octave and a sestet.

Bird-Count is an <u>English</u> sonnet. This is arranged in three quatrains and a final couplet, which has a different rhyme from the rest.

Winter Wedding is an <u>Italian</u> sonnet. This has an octave and a sestet, similar to the English sonnet but with ideas flowing from one line to the next. The ideas stop after the octet and start up again in the sestet.

Clearing Out the Hamster Cage is also an <u>Italian</u> sonnet but with a different rhyming pattern in the sestet.

Bird-Count

Today, for a survey, we're counting birds.
A flock's just settled on my patch – so hush!
We've divided the garden into thirds.
I've ticked off ten *sparrows*, a *blackbird*, *thrush*.

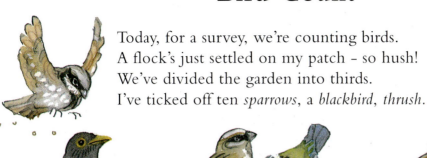

I scattered a handful of choice cake crumbs.
Two *bluetits*, and look! A *gold-crested wren*!
Behind where I hide a foxglove hums
with bees, I find *goldcrest*, pick up my pen.

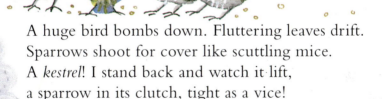

A huge bird bombs down. Fluttering leaves drift.
Sparrows shoot for cover like scuttling mice.
A *kestrel*! I stand back and watch it lift,
a sparrow in its clutch, tight as a vice!

I stare at the patch where the sun once shone
and ache, not knowing whose side to be on.

Winter Wedding

"Brr! Nothing between us and the North Pole,"
growled Aunt Anne. I wore a thick winter vest
under fancy clothes, and pinned to my chest
a carnation they called a buttonhole.
Hats went skew-whiff, skirts blew out of control
in raw winds. My curled fringe became a crest!
We posed for photos, every single guest:
eyes pale as pebbles and eyes bright as coal.

I stood beside my new cousins, two girls,
with shining black plaits. As the first snow fell
we stroked the bride's dress all covered in pearls.
Guests hugged warmly and wished the couple well;
silk saris fluttered, blown about in swirls,
the day Aunt Jill became Mrs Patel.

Clearing Out the Hamster Cage

Henry twizzles across the classroom floor
piloting his own roller coaster ride
in the safe see-through ball he plays inside
while we change his straw bedding: back and fore,
spinning round desk legs and bumping the door.
With so many nooks a bubble can hide
and his scampering claws our only guide,
trying to find him can prove quite a chore.

The wire door quivers and shuts with a *clink!*
We slide Henry gently back on the shelf
in a cage fit for a hamster wedding
with salad to nibble, water to drink.
But Henry's too fond of stuffing himself;
he digs right in and gobbles his bedding!

SOME COMMONLY USED TERMS

Stanza (or **verse**) Lines of a poem grouped together to make a pattern. Poems are formed of one or more stanzas. Each stanza is a kind of paragraph. Often stanzas will have the same number of lines and the same rhyme patterns. Sometimes a stanza is named because of the number of lines in it, as a couplet or quintet; sometimes the name comes from the poet who invented it, as the Burns Stanza.

Rhyme Words that match according to the way they sound. Only the initial consonant is changed, after which the words sound identical (jump/bump/thump). Rhymed words usually occur in patterns, and most often they stand at the end of a line. With rhymed words of more than one syllable, it is the stressed syllable that counts, and everything after it must match (forgiving/living).

Rhythm Even babies respond to rhythm: footsteps, songs, handclaps, running water, being rocked in someone's arms, a clock's tick. Poetry uses all these variations of rhythm and many more, from the strong to the less marked.

Simile This is a word meaning likeness. Often the best way to describe something is by comparing it with something else. In *Eclipse,* the moon is "round as a melon" to express its shape. Later it shrinks "like a perished balloon" to show the change in its shape.

Metaphor Another form of comparison, often not as obvious. At the end of *Eclipse,* the moon is compared to a potato without using the words "as" or "like". Sometimes a whole poem can be a metaphor.

Syllable A single unit of a word. Each syllable can be said by itself when a word is pronounced. For example, elephant has three syllables: el-e-phant; chicken has two; chick-en; cat has one.